New Red Chairs

Priscilla Mileski

Made with ❤ on the BookLeaf Publishing Platform
www.bookleafpub.in
www.bookleafpub.com

Dedication

To my crone friends.

Preface

2024 has been an extraordinary year of creativity and healing. The two go hand in hand.

Acknowledgements

Thank you to my editor, my daughter Madeline Mileski and to my friends for all the encouragement. Also to my online readers who shared many kind words. Hecate, you have been a catalyst in my writing - thank you!

Summer Solstice

1

Unable to attend
the Summer Solstice
at Stonehenge,
we make our own
from a quarry of
spongy gold pound cake.

We construct pillars and lintels
and mortise them with
sweet whipped cream.
Sugared strawberries
ooze their juices
down a sacrificial altar.

Our fingers are sticky
with the summer night
and a strawberry moon.

Frog Viewing

Tomorrow will be 85 degrees
with rain and thunder.
Let's stand on the
old wood bridge
and watch the frogs.
Let's feel the rain
and be frogs.

Dottie's Rain

"Oh, write a poem about the rain!
Drip, drip, splash, splash!" she says.
It's been in the 90s for days.
Last night Thor had his way
and today, in the late afternoon,
there are still puddles in the road
and tree branches hang heavy and low.

I go to the farm stand
where a basket of
purple-streaked eggplant
compete with red and yellow
tomatoes, green beans
and pink blush peaches.
And I appreciate the rain.

I stop to admire the precise
fields of tasseled corn, humid
and dense. The still-green ears
bent downward, soaked and raw.
Across the road, soybeans
anticipate the gold of Fall.
And I appreciate the rain.

Blackberry Picking on Banjo Lane

It's early and the air is steamy.
You put on long denim jeans
and head to Banjo Lane
for blackberry picking.

You have to imagine
the banjo beneath the bird song.
The blackberries are small
and the thorns are sharp.

But the kid in me remembers -
carefully check under the leaf,
cup the hand while you pluck.
The sweet ripe berry falls just right.

Give a Skink a Drink

5

Put a little
saucer
on your front
porch.
Add a couple stones.
Sit quietly and wait.

Five black lines
draw down her back
to her still intact
bright blue tail.

I'm hoping for skinklets.

Rudbeckia

Black-eyed Susan
crowds out any weeds
and offers her many sun
faces to the blue summer sky.

She is equally at home
along roadside ditches
or the front yard gardens
of backyard witches.

And if poetry serves her well,
Sweet William, home
from the seven seas,
dries her eyes and plants
his roots lovingly by her side.

The House Across the Lawn

The house across the lawn,
on the other side of the picket fence,
belongs to my neighbor.
She holds council in her living room.

Here her various visitors
sit to engage. A piece of cake,
a diet coke, needle and thread,
match and candle.

Memory and resolve
flow in and out the front door.
Friendships are seasoned
with German grit, craft
and a grateful laugh.

Zinnia

I tried the latest variety,
the Queen series.
Stately with tight, trim petals,
globes of blush pink and soft
moss green. Small and reserved,
they last quite long in a vase.

Alongside, the old bold
blood-red zinnias,
big as my fist, each with a gold
crown. Large open petals. Intense.
Fewer seeds but easy to harvest.
They are the red sun of each bouquet.

New Red Chair

Come sit with me
on the front porch
in the new red chair.

From here you can see
the sun-blessed, blood-red
maple tree seeds just
waiting for the wind.

And just now, a tailless skink
skitters across the concrete
just feet beyond my foot.
He circles the upright post
and the downspout.
He looks wonky without a tail
but he is alive.
And he rests in the shade
while I refill the water bowl
and place raisins on the rock.

Shed Rabbit

The shed rabbit
hangs out front.
She knows me well.
She sits very still
as I wander walk the yard.

She has persisted. Has been
safe in my well-shrubbed yard.
She will, once again, burrow
beneath the backyard shed
and she will have kits in the Spring.

Full Moon Evening

The boardwalk walks us through
marsh grass, cattails and feathered fragmities.
It is evening, the slanted sun
saturates the still-green grasses that
reflect along the estuary stream.

It's full moon and we've brought
sweet scented moonwater to bask
in the early moon rising.
The music on your phone turns
to feather flight and bone.

Two eagles circle, they call their song.
They flow low over us where we
sit on a bench, our heads thrown back.
They are curious about the music,
the calling of the flutes.

Rabbit Women

12

Come all ye rabbit women
spooky and calm in
your autumnal garb.
Come, claim your warren
of wildness, your boots,
your twitching whiskers.
Reign o'er the witch
festival of your pumpkin
field, freshen your lips
with pumpkin spice.
Take all that is yours.

The Path

Well-worn and unknown,
the wake of all that's done,
the lure of what's to come,
and all around, waves
cut deep by the ancestors.

Step lightly with keen observation,
barefoot intuition and
deep, abiding gratitude.
Carry the cloak of the goddess,
the candle, the knife.

Each step bears creation,
artful and nourishing for
all who will walk the path.

October Night

The nights have turned cool,
I stand barefoot
on the front porch.
It is still and quiet
under a crisp crescent moon.

The trees, the dark dense
shrubs, stand in shadow
poised with expectation.
The thin air, skilled as owl breath
is steeped with anticipation.

Beach

15

Full-moon Atlantic waves
sweep the beach clean to a
fine-grained bright white canvas.
Morning sun warms the wrack.

Waves crest, crash and break.
A scurry of shore birds
race. My shadow meets
the shadow of a seagull -
raised arm to open beak.

Winter Jacket

First night on the front porch
in a light winter jacket.
Pockets hold a story.
Two dog poo bags,
a neatly folded paper towel,
several silver Hershey Kiss
wrappers. Grungy lip balm,
a red silk ribbon,
some wadded up black
electrical tape and a smidgen
of bird seed. Ingredients for winter.
Samhain is near.

Spirit Tree

Barred owls
call softly where old yards
support older trees.

Each year the broad oak
cradles young owls deep
in its hollow.

We leave a thin red thread
round the trunk
of a spirit tree.

For May

On a picnic table
under a gazebo,
we share lunch and
watch the birds - seagulls,
migratory ducks,
a gray heron and an eagle.

A place where stream
meets river and takes
its journey out into
the open Bay.
We walk a bit to savor
the new November day.

Preparing for Solstice

We prepare for Solstice.
Firewood for Yule logs,
tall taper candles - red, green
and white. Ribbon and twine.
Dede will bring red-berried holly
and long-needle pine.

Glitter for pine cones
gathered from the park,
Playful gnomes, poems
of season, dark and light.
Spiced rum and eggnog,
peppermint tea for me.

Merry Meet and Merry We Will Be

Magnolia

Magnolia pods drop
just about now.
Brilliant red seed peeks
through the ancient
medieval armor that
holds and protects.

In the house, in a large blue bowl,
they rest, soon they will
dry and the red harvest
will pop. We can plant
them at the
edge of the wood.

Child

21

Child of crayons, sand
and mud
go and play
in safety and in love.
You are treasured.
You need no longer
protect or diminish yourself.
You rest in the arms
of your adult self
and she carries both
you and the Goddess.